J/649.122

LISKEARD
TEL.

2 4 FEB 1994   1 1 AUG 1995
1 4 MAR 1994
- 2 SEP 1994
2 7 SEP 1994

CANCELLED

- 2 MAY 1995

ALTHEA
The new baby
0285621203

CORNWALL COUNTY COUNCIL
LIBRARIES AND ARTS DEPARTMENT

Souvenir Press

The New Baby
by Althea
illustrated by Nita Sowter

Published by Souvenir Press Ltd, 43 Great Russell Street, London WC1B 3PA
© 1973 Dinosaur Publications Ltd ISBN 0 285 62120 3
Reprinted 1984, 1991
Printed in Hong Kong through Bookbuilders Ltd

It's very exciting
when your mother
is going to have a new baby.
Will it be a brother or a sister?

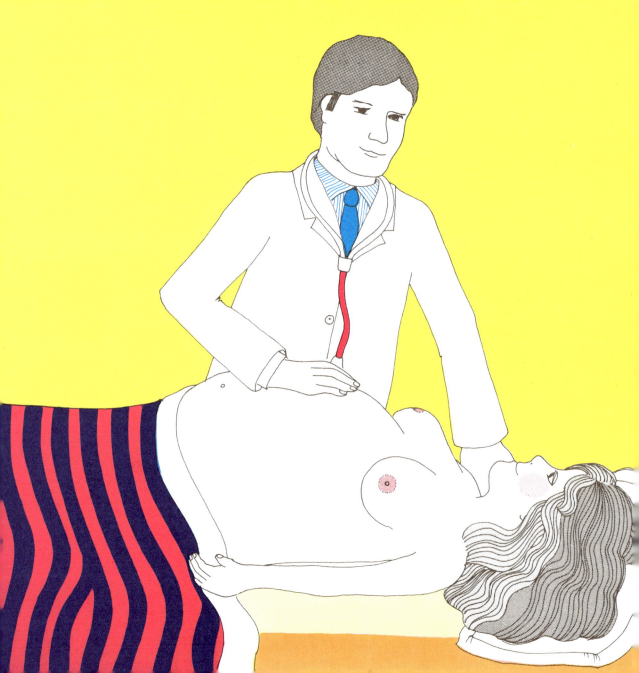

Your mother will go
to the doctor quite often.
He listens
to make sure the baby
is comfortable in her tummy.

When new babies are born
they are very small,
and they can't see very well.

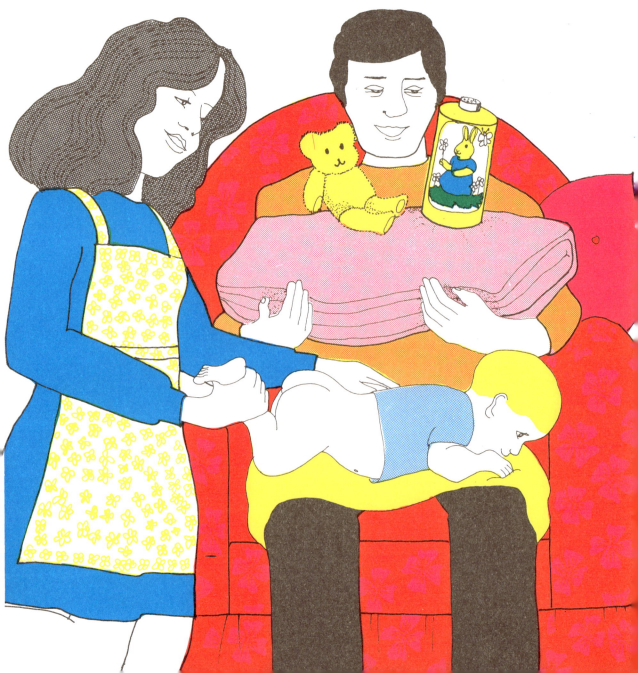

Babies need to be
looked after all the time
because they can't
do anything for themselves.

So you and your Mummy and
Daddy will be very busy!

They sleep a lot of the time,
and we have to be careful
not to wake them.

But they soon wake up and cry for food
when they are hungry.

At first, babies are fed only with milk. Some mothers feed their baby with milk which is made in her breasts.

Other mothers feed their babies with milk from a bottle with a teat fixed on it.

Babies need to have their nappies changed.

Usually they are bathed in a special baby's bath, or perhaps in a new washing-up bowl!

Quite soon the baby will
learn about smiling.
When you smile at him,
he will smile back again.

He soon begins to eat
other food as well as milk.

Babies need fresh air
so we put them outside in a pram,
or take them for a walk in it.

When they have learned to sit up,
babies like to watch you play.

We must be careful
which toys we give them, because
they put everything in their mouths!

After they learn to crawl
they will try to join in your games.

Sometimes they are a bit annoying.
They don't mean to be
but they are very curious.

We have to be very patient
and gentle, and teach them
how to play properly.